Beautiful stranger

By Anna Cellmer

First published in 2007 in Lulu Publisher

By Anna Cellmer

annaela3@gmail.com
http://stores.lulu.com/annaela3
https://www.facebook.com/pages/Daily-Crumbs-poetry-collections-by-Anna-Cellmer/152073201656457
https://www.facebook.com/opengatesbyAnnaCellmer
https://www.facebook.com/pages/Beautiful-Stranger-by-Anna-Cellmer/211403929016220
https://www.facebook.com/soundofsilencebyannacellmer
https://www.facebook.com/anna.cellmer
https://www.facebook.com/anna.cellmer.1

I dedicate this book to some beautiful man I met once on my way and who is still some sweet one for me

It's you my love to whom I belong forever

1- Invisible touch
2- I love to be in Love with you
3- I'm too busy for lover
4- A date with a devil one
5- Strangers
6- Touching words
7- Go one deeper
8- Not a stranger
9- New love
10- Scent of love
11- Games
12- Do you want love?
13- My lover just came to the site
14- Expectations
15- Let's build this dream
16- Stay within
17- All the truth
18- Inner fields
19- No named
20- Not disappointed I'm
21- Separate worlds
22- On the way
23- Internal words
24- Come to me
25- No need to see you
26- Little sign
27- I live for you now
28- I love to know this
29- Sorrow
30- Come tonight
31- Forgive me
32- Missing your thoughts
33- Patient girl
34- Don't ask me again
35- Forever apart
36- I'm sorry for black thoughts
37- Love creation
38- You who stayed
39- Your new girl
40- Where is your heart now
41- Agreement
42- I love you
43- Life and poetry
44- You miss me
45- It's for you right now
46- You get on me baby
47- Outcast
48- Ashes
49- Come back
50- You had to do it
51- Do you love me?
52- Love words
53- Daily misses
54- Don't worry about me
55- Lovely words
56- Sweet sexy words
57- You are this one
58- Why angry
59- Not a right place
60- You did something good again
61- Then we will know

Invisible touch

I have what I wanted
I'm killed by the sight
I was in love again but
You were outside
You couldn't say
I'm yours
You couldn't see my soul
You don't even know
This story of love
Which came to me
Some time ago
You don't care
What you lose
At all

I love to be in Love with you

It's so easily to leave alone
Another one who seemed to be
So interesting to speak with
It's so sweetly to came back
To you
Another time
The memories win the battle
With the reality around
I love this picture of you
Within my soul
Hidden, rooted so deeply
So true
I love to be in love
With you
Forever and ever
I do

I'm too busy for lover

Oh, Mr. Unknown
Do you think it's so easy
To find a real lover
I'm quite busy woman
Besides it's really hard
To find someone right
And even if I would
To find someone handsome enough
I'm a bit shy, you know
It's not so easy at all
To start anything so real
No, my friend
It's not to me, I think
So, let's dream
What do you think?
Do you like it?
Do you want this still?
I wish to start another dream
With you
You are quite interesting boy
so...
I don't know
Maybe I'm wrong
But it's just like that
I said
What I had to say
To you today and
I have to wait
For the answer now
So, bye bye

A date with a devil one

How it's nice then
To met you so well
You must know this fact for sure
That almost every natural woman
In this world
Wants to find a devil on her way
To take her heart away
To make the mistress of her for a while
To let her forget
About whole life
She has to take care about
Come to me then
Lover
Take my world away
Hold me
Kiss me
Take me
So wild
Sweetly
And dirty
As only you can
Deeply
Invade my soul
Just like this
To the end
Of this dream
I'm curious you still
I feel love in the air
This wickedly sensual
Scent of your horny sight
Inside
And I feel alright
Within you
So far

Strangers

Write me another piece like this
And you will stay the lover from my dreams
Stranger

Lord, how come you
Let me fall in love
With another one
Nice man who just came
And knocked to my door
Again

Strangers come and go
This is the way
They become the part of the story

Some of them are with me some of them are gone
This is the way the life goes on

Touching words

I shouldn't tell you a few things
But if you are not real here
It is without any sense to be
Touching words
Virtual world within
Seems to be
This special sound
Of life I need but
perhaps
It's without any sense
To anyone
So, why do I do this?
Why?
Just somehow it works
I wish to be yours tonight
Yes tell me that you want me
And call me sweetheart
You can stay this perfect lover
Is it not nice to each other?
Is it not right?

Go one deeper

If you are not going to fall in love with me
Then go away from my dreams!
Do you want me?
I don't think so
This what you want is just a little dream
But you don't want me in real
You don't expect anything, so
You have what you want
This short and flat bly bly
Between the strangers we are

Busy man, busy man
You don't have the time for love then
But do you know what the time is for?
You are so busy as you want
As you need and wish mostly
Are you the owner of your time?
Are you the master of your life?
Are you ready to go outside?
Are you able to drown
Within someone?

Not a stranger

You are not a stranger at all
Perhaps
Possibly you are this kindred soul
Maybe my friend
I think so
I can understand you
I like to walk through
All these daily human things
What else do I need
To believe
That you are this special gift
I get during a day
To enjoy, to write
To spend another while
With the smile?

New love

Watching for the signs of life
The dream I have had once
Alive
It's you who opened
My eyes again
For this primeval wish
Which I almost forget

It's you
Who I was looking for
It's you who I was dream about
I believe that all
Love I had before
Were just to know
How to speak to you
My love
To make you

The happiest man
On this world
I suppose

Scent of love

She is dreaming again
About her lover man
This one is
Much younger more pretty
And sweet
That she wants him so deeply
This love grows inside quickly
Her soul explodes one more time
She can feel him
Under the skin so warm
She owns him
Within her dream so fine
She is watching the signs

She catch all whiles
In the words he brings
She see the light
In the breath of delight
Inspired
By this world
He gave to her
In the air

Games

It's well to know what is right and what is wrong
choosing this what is good to you
occasionally just the moment through
but even if you know
that something is just an illusion
take this and don't lose the truth
all the pleasure of illusion's world is
in its fluency

Take me tonight deeply and free
I'm here for you
you can believe
even if we never
see each other

I can play with you
to love affair
taking a pleasure of it
to dissolve, to dipped into us but
I know that it is he
who's love is real
he is this one who stays by my side still
but I want you both
tonight, for a while, forever, whatever
our mild possession
devoid of big risk
because I'm here
you are there still
we just take a pleasure of our illusion
to inspire, to fly for a while
to rise this hunger for a special life
we all fight with the boredom outside
we play exciting games
to turn us on
to another day
living for a pleasure
for these moments we can catch
we can suddenly find

taming strangers
to create internal world
we can watch TV
it's almost this same but
less funny

My favorite game is to make
the stranger my friend

but these are
different kind of plays yet
friends become lovers
lovers become slaves
slaves become masters
masters become enemies
enemies become strangers

there is always some risk
between you and me

Another art is to devote yourself
in the name of idea
to everything you wish
God, policy, sex, pleasure, love
there is just one condition
in everything you do
you must be real
you have to be
able to drown
but of course
you can just slither on the surface
laughing
but it is never enough
to the one
who name himself the philosopher

Sometimes the family
is the key of true life too
you can built your life around
of this what you love, you care about
but sometimes the family
becomes this thing you want to escape of
to the world of illusions
it's not a bad world
just easy to crash
you can stay alone in the desert
trying to build your world again
but after years you don't have
so much force and enthusiasm as well
so there is some risk
your life' d stay empty enough

to let you feel bad if you can't
live for idea just

look positive
the light is better
than darkness
in a long distance
relationship
with the world

there is also like this
that we are going through
another step into the knowledge
if I'm the woman I know a bit more than the girl I was
if I'm the wife I know a bit more than miss
if I'm mother I know a bit more than wife
I'm mistress, I'm wife, I'm mother
everything is just process in progress
we turn into the wisdom of reality
we turn into experience
of our life

so jump into the life
Don't be afraid
this is the way
to fill your self

There is some story about life too
life is an empty glass
to fill
put the stones first
you can see the free space yet
so put the gravel in
not filled still?
put the sand
but don't put it first because
there wont be space for nothing else

Do you want love?

You can feed my soul by this love to you
But are you sure you can stand this, my love?
Do you have the time and place
In your heart
To let this feeling grow?
Are you sure you want love?
Maybe just take this beautiful body I own
And that will be enough?
Are you sure you want me whole?
You still have a choice
Because you are wonderful boy
Who I want

My lover just came to the site

You are here again
My lover just came
To the site
To this dream world
Which we have both
How I love to see
Your picture here
How I love to know
That you are so close
So touchable
Every day
So sweet with your
Heart and face
So familiar to me
Suddenly
My friend, my lover
Who will be mine
In the right time

Expectations

I don't expect
You'd marry me
No, my boy
This what I want
Is something much more
I'm going to make you
The slave of love

Let's build this dream

Perhaps all we have to do
Is just to build this dream
Is to live by this illusion
To dream our dream of love
To have more than we have now
To need each other as no one before
That's all we can do, my love
That's all

Stay within

It wasn't a long time ago
When you came suddenly to my world
But I don't remember
How it was before
How I could live without your soul
Please stay with me
Stay within
I feel good with you
Like this
I need you to live

All the truth

What the truth are you looking for
Just take me and you will see it
Within my eyes, baby
All the truth
Is this what turns you on
What makes you feel
This way as you feel right now
So happy with me somehow
So come on stop these silly talks
About the philosophical aspect of the world
About this special place which not exists at all
Don't say that you look for the challenge in me like this
Just come and take me
In your words, in your thoughts, in real
The way is the best for you and me
Occasionally or still,
No matter how you wish and dream
What kind of truth
Do you want to know more?
Just come and take me, honey
You've won me already
With this big lottery of thoughts
So you can have this what you want
You were brave enough
To stay my love

Inner fields

There is someone here who I can feel
but this distance between
I just feel him in the air
but it's sometimes hard to stand
I'm not good within my world
not known enough to understand
Where are you, my friend?
How to start conversation with such a man?
I don't know what to do
so I just write another piece
like this

Warm or cold, uptight, happy or just fine
you are so close I'm just in sight
I like to be like that
to feel you behind, to stay closer a bit
but I don't want to interfere your space
I feel you as a friend, and someone else
it's difficult to stand -you by me
when I'm not sure you want to be
so close to me as I wish

warm and cold the two aspects of my world
uptight relaxed, some feelings between
this two spaces
someone just came another gone
sad or happy
I'm going through this path
Just to be in sight
To stay by you
I don't need the crowd
I just want this right one
to whom I feel this special warm
this hunger within and trembling and need
to be with

games players
I was today the lucky one
because we were speaking for a while

and it's a reason why I'm happy today
I win my own play
The chosen one was with me
as I planned that it could be

several lines
feelings connection
changed interrupt
he just came he is gone
she is with him I can't be there
I'm afraid
he preferred to be with her
all these little touches
of the heart
jealous, fear, shy, uptight
I feel right now
playing within this game
on the fields of feelings
That are growing or dying around
I didn't expect this
how much of it can be within me
I'm so touched every time
He is not by my side, but with her
it's incredible, I'd probably die
from all these feelings around
If I wouldn't have anything else
in my life
but I have, so I can play this way
still, to feel, to win, to be

No named

If I can't call you
My lover
How I can called you then?
You closed the door to you
So, I'm where I'm
At the beginning and at the end
Of this simple story
About the woman and the man

Not disappointed I'm

Disappointed am I?
You said
No, honey
I'm not going to be like that
I have a faith
In this love but
Just sometimes
I have these whiles
When I realize
That all I have
Are just these
A few big words
Which you said
Some time ago
And your silence so far
But it's all right
My love
I know you are with me
Somehow
I know everything
Is going to be great
Because you know
That I love
And I know
That you want this
More and more

Separate worlds

How I wish that you would write to me
these words so sweet as you did today
to her for the one you love
for this who lights your night so bright
but I know that we live in these separate worlds
when I can't touch you and you can't touch me in real
where only our souls sometimes meet
and this is sometimes so hard to understand
that we don't have any chance
to be together
there is no way for us
outside this dream
but I still wish to live
within

On the way

You live inside
This dream which
I used to call
My life

We never know
Where this path
Leads us
And this is
The most exciting
Part of the story

Internal words

Sometimes I try to be hard
and not write for a while to you
To make you feel this way as you do
unsure
For a while
Is this love real
Are you in love with me still?
But my words are growing in me
And then I just can't
To not let you know
That I care that I want
you
I wont beg you for anything
I'm strong enough to not do it
But I miss your words
The sight of you
Momentarily I'm scared
That you go away but I know
That everything will be ok
I still have hope
For this special love
But if you ever decide to
Not start this in real
Please tell me
Tell me everything you think
I'm so hungry your soul
Within me
If you decide to go away
I'll understand
I'll be sad
But life is like that
And we both must want
This same
To make this love
Great

Every day with you inside
Is like a new way
new beginning, another start
We can say hello
and we can say goodbye

I have had this dark thoughts
From time to time
That you don't care
That you would stop it and go away
But then
I can't, I can't stop my self
I wish to have you
Someway
Even with your stillness
And when you are so silent
Even if you don't come to me
And if I wont come to you
I still want to be with you
And I can't play with you
In silence game
To let you
Be hungry me
more
I'm not able to do that yet
So forgive me
That I let you know again
That I'm with you
That you are my man

Come to me

I don't need your words
My lover
I don't need them anymore
I just want you to come to me
To go on this dream
Which start some time ago
So, come to me soon
My love
Come to me in real
I wish to be your girl
I wish your fingertips on me
I dream about you within
So come to me soon
I'll remember you
All my life through
You can be sure

No need to see you

Through all these years
I've been learning only this
How to run away
From you
And how to come back

You still live there
But I can't meet you again
You can have another one
So I should be careful
And walk away
From your door
Before you could come

And this is all right
I don't need to
See you again at all
I just had to know
Are you still here
Close to my world

Little sign

I don't have
Courage enough
To see you again
But it's good to know
That you are still here
So close
It's good to know
That everything
Is all right with you
I hope I didn't touch you
Too much
I hope you didn't have
A hard night
Because of this
Little sign

I live for you now

I live for the feeling
Like this
I have right now
From the time
You came to my life
So suddenly
I live for the man
As you are
I live for this night
I could spend
Within your arms
I live for the charm
Of these words
You gave to me so far
So sweet so wild
I live for you now
And for this
What can be
between you and me

I love to know this

How I love to know
That you are my man
That you are my love
How I love to see
The words of you so sweet
To me
How I love to wait
When I know that you will come
Soon
To give me so much pleasure
To give me so much joy
How I love to be yours
How I love to believe
That you will come to me
For real

Sorrow

Sometimes I think
That if I'd reach
Only for you
To come to me
I'd probably die
From sorrow
That you don't come
That all I see
Is just an empty space
Where you should be
So I have to
Keep whole the world
During this time
When you have been gone
When I'm waiting for you
Alone

Come tonight

Yes you're right, my love
We don't need to hurry up at all
We have a lot of time
To meet each other
Step by step
We will know more and more
That you would fill my soul
To complete me whole
I don't want to disappoint you
Not at all
I just love to hear your voice
I just need to be sure of it
That you feel the same
What I feel
That's why I write
All these things
But I believe
That you want me still
And I have hope
For this love
Which wont disappoint
Anyone

I'm so hungry of your words
I'm curious of your soul
Your point of view
For the things
Your relationships
Your life which you live
As much as your touch and kiss
As much as your palms and lips on me
I want you whole in me
Please complete me
Be within
This is my dream
But you know
That I wish still
To have your heart
So I will try
To be this right girl
If you wish
Even living here
Within your dreams
About me
I wish to make you happy

And I know you want this same
And I love this
I want this
I need
So, please come to me
When I'll go to sleep
Come to my dream
I need to feel your touch inside
I wish to hold your mind
And kiss you for good night
Tonight

Forgive me

You are silent
It always makes me a bit sad
Especially when before that
I had written something what
I regret
When I'm too emotional
To you sometimes,
When I have my black thoughts
or doubts,
And I have put them all to you
Then this silence,
Then I feel
Such an emptiness
Such a idle day,
You blend into me as a tree
I'm not sure how I could live
Without you
I don't want even to imagine this
You are within me
And it's enough to live
And to feel
Everything
What is possible
And to love you still
Forever and ever I will
And forgive me
Every doubt
I have had so far
Every bad word
Every thought
Which is against
Our love,
You and me,
Which is because
I feel so weak
Sometimes
Without your arms
Around me

Missing your thoughts

The whisper of love
Came to my soul again
But I'm not sure of your heart
Still
As I know you
And this
What do you want
The most
My Dear

Perhaps you don't have
Whole my heart yet
But it doesn't mean
That you can't take me tonight

I'm suspicious still a bit
But it doesn't mean
That I don't love you
Because I do
Yes I do

It's just that
I'm still unsure
This what you hide inside
I'm still afraid that
You and I it's just a dream
Which can't exist in reality

By the way

You make my days so full of life
You make my heart so full of smiles
I'm so glad to find you

but

How I wish to be sure
That we can survive the time
All this time
When we are not together,
Do you think of me still
Even when I'm silent
Even when you are silent,
When we don't see
We don't touch each other,

When we don't see our thoughts,
When we do so many things around
And we don't know anything about this?
I need your words as an air
Please come and say
That you love me
And you care
I don't like it that
When I'm silent
You are like this too
At this time I'm afraid
Our love is not growing at all
At this time
We can stay strangers again
You and I can disappear
I don't want this
I feel good with you
I feel as a part of your life
As a part of you
But these whiles
When I'm not sure
Annoying me a bit
But I can't do anything

Where are you?
My love?
And why so little time
You can spend with me,
Why you don't want
To share your soul freely
You don't need
You don't feel you have to, perhaps
But I miss your words
I try to live normally
And enjoy other things
But I miss your thoughts
And I'm afraid of this love
I don't want to lose
Something so special, so good
I get from life again,
So please don't let me think
This way
Come and say
That you live, that you think
And you are with me still
In this dream

Patient girl

Patient girl
Is waiting for a man
To come
But she can't be so alone
So she is adored
At this time by someone special too
Who wants to take her heart and soul
But she doesn't know what to do
She knows that she loves
The man who
Is absent so often
and she needs more daily care
so she lets another came
To her mind and heart too
What to do
What to do
Does she lost
His this way?
Does she stay alone
At the end?
I don't know
But I want
You
I want you the most
But you can't be by my side
All the time
You are too busy for that
So, I have to do something
With this free time
To not die
To stay alive
For you
Caring lover
Is this
What she needs the most
But he can't come
To her world again
He is silent
He is impossible man
But the best for her

Don't ask me again

What is this what are you asking for
Do you want words of love without love?
What do you mean by this
It kind of trick must be
I know you want that I'd think about you more
This is the reason of your wish so strange
This is the need of you to be with me
Even like this

Or maybe you think that this way
I'll start to love you
Living again
Within my own world of words
But it doesn't work like this at all
Such art for art doesn't have any sense
I need to love first to write about this
Any improvement I can't find
In this idea of empty light

Better to die in the cold ocean could be
Than listen me

No my friend I can't do this for you
I wont feed your soul
These words which I can't feel
I wont tell you these lies sweet
It's not a point to make it this way
Only real thing can be ok
Only real love can bring us joy
So don't ask again
About words of love
Which I couldn't say from my heart

Forever apart

It seems that
This what you want
My love
Is just to whisper
To my soul
Your sweet words
To make me believe
In this dream
Which you never want
To make real
But I forgive you
I wish to dream
All my life then
So, do what you want
If you only know
How to make me alive
You can stay here
Within my heart
Forever and ever apart

I'm sorry for black thoughts

I'm sorry my love
I shouldn't accuse you
Just like this
Especially right now
When you are ill
I shouldn't be so angry
Because of something
What is not perhaps depended of
Anyone
I'm sorry to be like this today
You see I'm not even able to try to leave you
I was just so full of these sad thoughts
That you don't care of me
One more time I doubt
Once again I did this
I stopped to believe

I still hear your words
'Never ever questioning my love to you'
But it's so hard sometimes It's so hard
My love
To believe that you care
When I don't see this
When everything is against
You and me

Why do I feel this sorrow
Because of this what
Didn't happened

Why

I don't know
But now
Please believe me
I want you to live here
I don't feel well thinking that I could stop
No I don't want to leave at all
I just wish you could
Care a bit more just a bit
Just don't be silent too long
That's it

Love creation

I've learnt how to
Not hide this
What I miss

I've seen this
In my heart
What I lack

I've built
This world
Which can be
The essence to live

And then you came
To show me
What the love is

And then you filled
This open dream
I use to live in

To make it real

The guest of mine
Arrived and now
I have to learn
How to share this world
I've built

To create the new dream
About you and me
To live and to feel
The new space
And the new reality
In you
In me
In the place
Within

To make our hearts
So happy and shined
Just to make us alive

You who stayed

I place my thoughts
Before the sight of you
Searching this longing
I have still inside
Looking for the man
As you are
I find my self
In an empty space
Of wanting
Lost in the world
Which is just a flash
Of touching words
Floating from your minds
Across the light of my screen
The window is open wide
For all of these rays of smiles
Curiosity is a guider of mine
So I'm still looking around
To another one small world of your own
To catch to feel to feed my soul
But only you is this one
Who stayed for good
To belong
To want
To love
To waiting for

Your new girl

You don't even know how it hurts
such words, but don't worry about
It's just because I love you
I think I'll be fine soon, I hope
It's just for a while I feel so bad
Like all the world just become gray
from now
when I see that you are not mine
that you just found another one
girlfriend to love
but thank you
that you are so honest with me, my love
I was afraid that this dream is too good
and that someday
something will happen like this
something wont be just as i wish
but i know that it's not possible
to live just like this with me
I know I understand
your need to be with some real warm girl
by your side
but today you just realized me again who I'm
I'm just married and mother
living so far away from you
I can't give you this what she can do, I'm sure
So maybe I should just go away with all this love
to leave you in peace with another one
I just feel so sad now but I understand
I wish you the best
I hope you are ok
If you ever need me
Let me know
I'm still here for you
But I think that I should
Just leave you alone right now
I think I should leave you
yes I think
Yes I'll try I promise
I'll try to not be sad
because of this fact
that my perfect man
have a new girlfriend
from now
yes I'll try to survive
but how to believe in your words of love

how to understand clear
I'll try to live with this somehow
but I wont fight
I don't have the chance
to win with the reality

but come back to me
when you will need me
come back when you will be free
and for me
goodbye for now
my sweet man
goodbye
don't think about me too much
it wont be good for your new girlfriend
for this new relationship which you start to build
try to be happy with her
just remember
That I'm where I'm
Just enjoy your new love
forget about me
God how I'm sad telling this
A pity girl
but maybe tomorrow I'll be fine
and I'll understand better
and I'll try to smile
but for now
I can't I'm sorry I can't
It was just too beautiful
that It could be real

but you know that I wish you the best on your way
don't forget me
don't forget

I know it was hard to you
to live with this love alone
but now
it's so hard to me
To live with this fact
that you have a new one
but I'll try
Yes I'll try
Just can't stop these tears fall down
right now

Where is your heart now?

I love you,
Yes you are right
Nothing has changed between us darling,
I've had just this sad night
Because of this what you said to me recently
It's hard to me sometimes
To find out again this reality around,
Yes you need someone by your side,
Maybe I don't like my life at all
But I don't know how could i change this now
I lived in this dream about perfect love
And now I have to wake up for a while
Everything is good if we feel both good with this so
I'll try to accept you new life and love now
oh
But it was just a week ago
When you said
That you are mine
That you love me
And that I should remember this
Always
How it is now
My sweet
How it is
Where is your heart
Placed
Where it is?
Tell me please

Agreement

You just killed one dream
That I'd leave for you
my home
but I still can find another one
dream to live by
you just turn this love
into simple affair
but it's OK
I can live with this
I suppose
maybe it's even better dream
for both
yes my love

I love you

I love you
And this is so natural
I love you
And I can let you go
I love you
You live within my soul
I love you
And I smile knowing this
I love you
And mostly I miss you too
I love you
And I don't need to touch you
I love you
And this is enough to feel you
I love you
And I feel your words this special way
I love you
And I'm ok even if you are so far away
I love you
And it doesn't matter what you do
I love you
And you can love someone else too
I love you
And you can go wherever you want
I love you
And I can meet on my way whoever I do
I love you
And this is some kind of absolute
I love you
And the time doesn't matter anymore
I love you
And this is like a faith in a god
I love you
And I feel joy and calm in my heart
I love you
And this is like a dream I have
I love you
And you live here within me
I love you
And this sounds like music in my mind
I love you
And nothing can change this I suppose
I love you
Even just as a voice I hear still within me

I love you
And it's going on
I love you
And it's good to know this truth
I love you
And this is like a whisper to my soul
I love you
And this keeps me alive
I love you
And every time I think of you
I love you
And there is no need inside me anymore
I love you
And this love is pure right now
I love you
And this is fine

There is open space between us darling
I know
There is freedom that makes our love grow
There is time
That makes it eternal
There is a world
Where we choose our own path to go
There is life
That brings to us new lovers and smiles
There is place
Full of changes and surprises
Every day but this
What is between us
Never change
Even if it has many faces
And even if we can see each other
In many different ways
And this is a miracle
That makes our life beautiful
So, fly my angel of love
Fly to the beauty of this world
And let this life makes you happy and full of joy
But stay with me by your thoughts and mind
To feel me forever inside
And I'll be there
Wherever you will need to see me
And I'll support everything
You wish to do or to have too
And I'll stay here for you
Whenever you will need to come

So be free as much as you can
As much as you want
And be my love
Forever

You gave me freedom and
My love will fly to you
On the wings of desire

Life and poetry

poetry
warped scraps of reality
raised on summits of thoughts
dressed into forms perfect less or more
to amuse, to believe, to feel, to penetrate furtively
into this what we call an existence

life
Is just this what flows
among one and the second line

You miss me

I love to feel you
This way
As I do today
After your words
Always so sweet to me

I love to hear
Your voice
I love to know
That you miss me

Darling
I love you
Still and
I want you
More and more
Every day
And I'm glad
To come back
To you
With whole my body and soul
I love to be yours
As you know

Never forget about this
My love

You miss me
That's all I need
To feel you
Inside me

It's for you right now

You say you love my poetry
You say you read it
you eat it, you drink

Maybe it's just because
I put my heart
To every word I write
And you know too
That most of it is for you

I came to this world
To make you happy, you know
To make you my man, my friend
and my lord

So, enjoy

You get on me baby

Such a simple word
"I miss you"
But how much to enjoy
I feel this so merrily within
It's such a pick to my soul
Such little word
Which makes me yours
I can't run away
From you, my love
One your word
And I'm back
To you
From my tour
Not important how far
I was for a while
From you
But always in sight
Of your heart
I'm yours
So happily yours
Whole my body
Is so soft for you
Just wanting
To be touched
How you make me feel this way
My boy
How you are doing this
I don't know
But I love
And I'm so glad
That you come.

Outcast

You don't want me anymore
So why do you want to read me still
If you don't need me
If I'm not worth of your love so suddenly
If you just scrap me on the floor
Like a broken doll
Which doesn't work anymore
As you want

You don't want me anymore
You don't believe in my love
So why do you want to read
My words
It's all broken right now

You don't want to see me on your site
You don't want me in your life
So don't take a pleasure
From my write
From my poems to you
If you don't want me anymore
My words are like me
So go away from my dreams
About this love for whole life
We could live with
Leave to the end
Me
Never come back
I can't stand another
Goodbye from your side
It's simply too hard.

Ashes

I left my lover
I left my friend
The man who loves me
So much and deep
I didn't love him
Enough to stay I think
Yes I wanted
I wanted you for a while
You are so sweet to me
But without him
I can't
I just can't
Be with you again
As you wish to

I can't love anymore
I'm broken
Not able to see
To feel, to live
I do not exist
He is gone
He is gone
He doesn't love me now
I can't stand my self
In his eyes so hard to me
He doesn't want me
Doesn't respect
Doesn't believe
That I'm worth one his breath
I'm leaving now
I'm not able to love
He is gone
His heart is cold for me
He closed the doors
Any way I can't see
By one cut
He destroyed all joy of life
All love I have had
To the world
So I can't
Let you to come in
There is only ashes
Which stay
For today in me

Come back

Just come to me
You don't have to
Love me anymore
Just come
And make love to me
Then you can go
Forever
He wont come
Here
I love you

**"I love you
The problem is
That you talk to another man**

**You told to another man
Come inside me"**

It's not truth
I never said these words
To another
I let him go
I don't want another man
Just you I want
He wont come
To me
Come back, please!
I can't live without you
I can't live

You had to do it

You had to leave me
I know
You had to do it
And now
I love you
More than ever
And now
I'm yours
Forever

Do you love me?

Do you love just me?

"You and my son"

Did you really want to leave me?

"...................................."

If I don't send you my message
That all I want is you,
You wouldn't do this
You will never send to me
Any message anymore?

"...................................."

Have you been waiting for my message to you?

"Yes, yes, yes!"

God, how I love you

**"I had to leave you when you mentioned about another man
Never ever have one"**

So it's you who are the man of my life

"I'll come soon to be inside you

How much I wish to kiss you now

Love words

You have my artistic passion
And you have my love
What do you need more?

"Your body"

Then come

"I'm coming to you"

Oh, god
My body
You want
How I'm happy
To hear your words
You always know so well
What to answer
Of my questions
Lover

You talk to me
As I want
That's why
I love you
As no one before
How I'm glad
You want
My body more
Than my love
and art
That's what
I wanted to know
To love you more
This night

It's so easy to become
Impatient again
From two days
I'm thinking
About you here
Because of your words
So sweet

I'm coming to you
And now I'm not sure
Are you coming just right now?
Or in the future we will have
Someday

And again
I'm so hungry you
Your eyes
Your hands
Your lips on me
And you within

I've found some new possibility for us
Some place unknown
But I do not want
To interrupt
In your life
I've learnt to wait
For you
I do not want
To interrupt
In this dream
I enjoy
Just my thoughts
About you
I don't need to talk
I don't need to call
To tell you this
But I still wish
To share with you
Some of these thoughts
Like before and I love to wait
For the signs
From your side
I love
When you are coming
To my world
So suddenly
I love my reactions
Of this
It's amazing for me still
Discovering this love
Inside my body and soul
It is wonderful

Daily misses

I'm dying again
Life is so empty today
He is silent from two days
It's hard to stand

But he is back
And this is good
He is back in the way
He could
He is always to me
Occasionally
But loving still and only me
As he said
And I believe again

Love makes me not able
To do anything again but
I can't forget about love
I can't
And I'm in this strange condition during a day
External life doesn't exist
I wish to look at his picture that's all I wish
And wait for him
Months or years
Doesn't matter
And never wake up from this dream I have
I'm writing to him
When I feel I must
I write a poems too and that's enough
And I learn how to be patient in love too
As he wants me to be right now
He creates me from the start
Because I forget my self
I forget the world and the life
I have one direction from now
To be in his arms
Someday
Only this has some meaning to me
Anything else
Is just a dream

Don't worry about me

You turned your back on the crowd
But remember
That here is the heart
Which is beating for you
So never mind
And come back to me soon
I'll be waiting for you
Whole my life through
I'm not impatient now
You know that
You have my heart
So you can go away
For as long as you need
As long it is necessary,
Don't worry about me
I know how to feed my soul
By smiles beauty and love

Lovely words

Sexy message
I received
From you today
So do it all
It wont be difficult
To you
I suppose
I love your words
You make me
Wanting you
So easily
So softly
And so good
You are doing this every time
You come here
My love
Except these whiles
When you
Are just leaving me
Or when you talk about
Another girl
You were busy with
Recently
But if you only come here
To make me yours
I'll be screaming for more
I'm sure of this
My boy
You are still the best
Lover I have
So come just
And take and do
What you are talking about
From some time.

Sweet sexy words

Sweet sexy words
I hear
From your mouth
And it makes me feel
So wonderful
So happy
And so wanting you
My boy
Every little word
Of yours
Is like a prayer
Is like a song
To my soul
I can feed my self like this
And live
And believe
And dream
About this holy night
Which will come
Soon
In the shadow
Of another day
Which just flowed away
With joy
That you share with me
This special dream
And that we live
So beautifully
We are the lucky ones aren't we?
We have everything
Love, desire and this special joy

Which the woman can give the man
Which the man can give the woman
In love.

You are this one

I love you

"And I do
You are my darling"

So simple loving words between us
Which only we can feel so much

How I love to receive all these lovely answers
Of yours

You are my soul mate
You are my sweet man
I wish to be so close to you
I love to know that I'm yours

I feel you near me
And I'm not afraid
To tell you anything
And I know
You'd understand me well
And I'm sure
Your words are true
You read my soul
And you perfectly know
What I want
You are this one
I was looking for
So long.

Why angry

Don't be so angry for me
The new man I have been met recently
I don't understand
Why so hurry you are
In this way to me
You are impossible
Emotional, passionate
And I'm afraid a bit
You in my life
I don't know
What to expect from you
What you are going to do
To say to me soon
You are amazing but
I love some other guy
And I can't promise you
That I'd be for you
Someone more than
This little ray of the sun
Which brings you smile
This I can be but
Someone more?
I can't be your lover
If you wish so
I have another man
Worth to wait for

Not a right place

As more I listen all these
Things
As more I want
Just one
I wish to be
In your arms
Open and warm
To me
Nothing more I need
But will you care of me?
Your life is so busy so complicated now
You don't have time enough
To have me all
So just stay like this
Live in my dreams
Just keep the touch
Just believe
Just be when I need
Your sweet words
I have to be strong
In life
I suppose
I need to realize
All these things I have
Until my boys grow up
And then
We can meet
And then we can be together
For a while
Or forever

You did something good again

If there is a heaven
Above the sky
For sure
There is some
Nice comfortable
Apartment there
For you
You did something
so good again
I'm proud of you
My old friend
And I wish you the best
In everything you do
Because all of this
Is so good
You are kind of
Angel in this world
And it's so nice
That there was a time
I have had a chance
To touch you
And to fall so deep
In you
Yes
Thank you
and good luck
With your Open Mind
and this
Charity festival
of Polish culture and art
In Jersey Land
For children health
Prepared
For better future
Of all of us
With smiles

You proved once again
That you can change the world
By your self
My friend

Then we will know

I think that life
Is not so simple at all
And if you've even promised
Me something
You don't have to keep this
If you don't really feel
That you want after a while
I'll understand this
My beautiful man
You know that I think
You are wonderful one
You know that I want you to come
But I realized again
That life is open wide
Just before your sight
And maybe this way is wrong
And maybe I'm too old
And not this right woman
To you at all
I'm afraid I'd complicate
Your life and your world
I'm afraid I start to love you now
And I don't want
That you regret anything
Especially this
That we have met
And that we feel so good with it
There is so many
Wonderful girls in this world
You should go to them
You should go and try
Them all
And then you can
Come back to me
If you will feel still
That you want this
And you need
Yes then comeback
And I'll understand you
Without any word anymore
And we will just hold each other
And kiss
and we will know
We will know
What love is

Believe in dreams

Do not kill dreams you believe in,
Embrace it

Even if some just have gone
Let moments of joy to fill you all
And relish it

Caress your mind by beauty and smile
And live by this every day
Do not murder hope
For something special which will come
Soon

Just believe and smile

And wait a while

And you will have it

Good bye and hello

Yes my love
I think I'll be always in love
With you
I'm glad I just can see
Your beautiful face
On this virtual space
And then I smile
To you
To my thoughts too
Even if now I'm more sure
That we wont see each other
Maybe for another year
Or more
I'll dream about your touch
All my life perhaps
But it's all right
I use to live like that
Mental life is as strong
Or even more
As this reality around
So we can stay as we are
Just here
Inside
So, good bye
And hello
My love

Normal day

And another date of your coming here
Just flowed away
Did I believe this time?
Yes a bit
I put some skirt
And stockings
On me
And I was thinking
What I'd do if you call
Suddenly
And I smiled
But in the deep of my heart
I knew
That you wont come
This time
So I didn't change any plans
I have had
It was just normal day
As every other
But I still believe
That you are
With me
As always

Love knows no distance

Once you said
To me
What are you doing here
Anna
Be realist
I'm living in the South
You are there in the North
So how come you see
The future for you and me?
Come back
To your home
There is no
Distant love
Possible

And now
When I know
Your answer for my call
I'm just more sure
That there is no
Any distance important
For true love
You were wrong

My new love
Who has found me
Lives much far
From you
But it doesn't matter
For us at all
We feel this
What you never did
And we are happy
To be together

You will never know
What you have lost
I suppose
But it doesn't matter anymore
Everyone has it's own true
To believe
And I hope
That you are happy

To gain this what you have been built
Your reality you live within

I'm happy living in my dream of love
Being there with my boy
Who always so perfectly knows
How to make me wanting him
On and on
He is the artist of my soul
He is the man who I know
Even without any real touch
He offered me
Much more
He made me
The woman in love
So, there is no other true
To me
Just that I love him
There is no other answer
That you never did
But who cares of this now?
The past has gone by
And now
Is just the heart which believes again
And there is new treasure to gain
And there is a dance of love
For this one
Who loves.

It doesn't hurt so much

No you don't hurt me
This time too much
That you didn't come
Maybe because
There is natural
In us, that every time
It disappoints less
Besides I bought some new dress
So I can say
I'm in good mood today
Yes, just a little bit regret
Not even this that you didn't come
But this
That I believe less
In every word you can say
From now
By the way
Why you didn't come
This time?
I wonder if you explain
In some interesting way
This fact that
You fool me again
I hope just that you make fun
With this game
You call by big words sometimes
But now I know
That you just play
But it's ok
It's good to laugh
We don't have the time for sorrows
It's without sense to worry
About such things too long
I'm just not going to take your words
Seriously
So, yes love me more
And forever
Be my boy
And feel good with these sweet lies
Which makes us fools sometimes

Why?

Nothing stayed from my passion today
Lovers - go away
I feel sadness inside
I want to be alone tonight

Why, why I miss your lies
So much?
Can I live without them
Anymore?
What is sweeter than
Your words

To me?
But how to listen you
If I don't believe

Why some of it
Still sounds so real
In me?

Why if you show
Nothing but
That you just play
With my heart
Why you do that?

And why I can't
Free away my self
From you
Why do I love you?

Your eyes are sad today

Your eyes seem so sad today
What do you feel, are you ok?
Is this that you are embarrassed still
You cant speak with me or it's something more?
Maybe I have hurt you by last letters, I know
You didn't expect such news
But I cant hide anything I live by
Other way it seems no sense
To be with you if you couldn't accept
All thoughts I run for
But what is in your mind now?
What is the new dream you are looking for?
Can't I share it with you anymore?
Is it something wrong between you and me?
What does your silence mean?
I don't want to guess, my love
I prefer to believe that this what was before
Is still here living inside
To burn again someday
In the right time
In the right day
Just to see your eyes in smiles
Again.

Intelligent you like

You like intelligent women
You said once oh
Am I strong-headed enough
To be your love?
What if all I have to offer to you
Is nothing but my fragile heart?
And my body so hungry you
Do you think it's enough?
What if I'm nothing but a simple girl?
And there is nothing so mysterious in me
To discover, to go deeper for?
What if I'm nothing but me?
Is it enough to you
Is it enough to love?
What if it can be nothing but a while
Even worth to remember
But there is no way to leave the past
To change our lives
Is it worth to start?
Is it worth to risk?
Do you want
To be in love with me
The way we are
Is it enough to fly
To be happy like this
Is it enough to live?
Oh why so many question all the time
If I love you and this is enough
To be so happy and to keep this dream
Just come someday
And touch me
And be for real

What if?

What if I lost my job?
My husband leaves me
My children stop love?

"Then I'd marry you"

Why so happy I'm
Right now?

I never thought
That marriage is something
Special in life
But you know
That from your mouths
It's so beautiful
Declaration of love

So, I don't need to worry
About the future now

How life is bright
How it is good
With you
As I said before
You always know
What to answer
Of my silly talk
To make me so happy
And to stop
All dark thoughts
That comes

Never doubt

What ever I say sometimes

What ever I do

Never doubt

In my love to you

And don't let me doubt

In you

Let me believe at this dream forever

That's all I want

All I need from you

now

Slide show

Every kind of silence
That I knew so far
Is nothing compared to yours
The way you speak to me right now
Teasing all my senses by little changes
On your site
Just another innocent picture you put there
Makes me insane makes me wanting to be
On the other side of you
On the other side of your dream
When you look at me
The way I see this here
The way I wish to live
Inside your mind still
And I'm so unsure
Who is the author of this
Slide show
That I wish to know
More

Who is this man I love so much?

The new pictures of yours I saw again
If not your call just a moment ago
It'd be again so hard to believe
That you can love me
I'm afraid you now a bit
I'm afraid that you cant really love one girl
But maybe it's just too much I see
Too much I feel to much I wish to have
You are free on your way, as always
I'm here just watching you
Feeling the man I wish to be with
But it's hard to stay self confident enough
To be the woman you could really love
I don't want to look this way
I wish to be just understanding girl
Looking positive for everything
Even for the fact that you have a good taste in that,
Yes some are really beautiful but what do they lack
That you need more all the time
That you just play with them or you watch
But you cant fall in love or maybe you do - with all?
Womanizer, who is this man I love so much
Who is this man I wish to touch and
Why I'm so attractive to him still,
Why he say that he loves me
Yes beautiful body is not all perhaps
You need some other things I have
or maybe you are tired a bit
of all this you can get so easily,
Yes good hunter you are, I think
You know that I also like this in you
Yet it's very hard sometimes to me
Especially now when I'm in love
When everything is so touching
Everything you do like this, to tease me
When I can see all your life here

I know I shouldn't it's not like that
Besides I'm not the angel as well
And I did in my life some things too
I met some boys on my way through,
Just never did any pictures of it.

Oh baby no I can't doubt in you and in me,
We should be together I think, because
I cant find any man so far
So attractive to me and so sweet as you are
I just know one I have to be strong
Sometimes more
Because it's not easy thing this love
It's touching too much
But from the other hand
I love even this freedom you have within
I'm always impressed of you, my man.

I'm just slave of love

I turn back into the madness
No escape from my mind
When I see your picture
And I feel your basic charm
I used to this silent impact
On my daily moods
Your play of emotions
Where I love to be drowned
Another battle within I started
To let you win
I'm just the slave of love
To let you be mine but
When I try to get the prime
I find my self in the life of illusions
To feel that you listen my voice
And I cry to you
To be so lost for a while
I don't know if you want more
Or you have enough
Of another storm or the weakness
Which go one
And me bared to you waiting in my room
I never know your side of this
Until I feel again your touch within me
Until you say you are with me still
On the other side of my mind
On the other side of this dream
What invade me to you
Are invisible chains of love
You don't even have to tie me up
To have me beside your heart
To own my soul and my wish
And to be here still
There is no any escape
From the room I came
Where I feel that I'm yours
And you are my man.

Life with or without you

Life is so enjoyable
When I feel you beside me,
Life with silence lost its charm
For a moment
And I turn in kind of torpor
Just to survive another day
Somehow,
I can even smile
I can be still so cheerful girl
To everyone
But inside me
I'm waiting
I'm waiting for any sign
From you
And I don't need to do
Anything else
I miss your touches
Only you know
How to touch me
Still so deeply, tenderly
That I could want you
Every day
That I'd dream to be
A part of you someday.

I'm sorry

I'm sorry if I disappointed you,
I'm sorry if I did something
What could touch you too much
I hate my self for this right now
But baby I just hope
That you can forgive me this
And let it gone with the wind

Until you are here
Even silent
I believe that I'm still
Close to your heart,
I don't' want to think
Another way
I don't want.

Maybe you need some free time
Maybe you know that this space is again too big
Between you and me
Maybe you don't want this so intensively
If you know that we need to wait
Maybe years
And you know that so many things
Is around still

I just don't know why I had to be like this
And I did some things that could make you sad
And full of doubts perhaps,
I'm ashamed of this but please forget it if you can
I wont do this again
I did so much mess between me and you
I'm so sorry for this, my love.

My love if I'm silent today
It means just that I'm so happy to know
Your heart never changed
That we live forever together in our dream
That you need this so much as me
That you belong to me
I just cuddle my self
In warm of your words
To make me sure again
That I'm yours
Still and all you wish
Is to be here with me

I'm beside you still

You may not feel my touch
Laying in your bed at night
After your always busy day
When you are tired

You may not see me
Watching your sleepy eyes
Just beneath your losing dream
When you are waking up

You may not share with me
Some of your daily things
You simply live by
During your cheerful life

But remember
That no matter what you do
And if things are going
Up or down
You can be sure
That I'm here
For you

My heart never lies to me
So you know
That I'm always beside you
And I feel with this so good
That nothing can change
This simple truth
That I belong to you

And that there is nothing
More precious on this world
To me
Than our story of love
And our dream we drowned both
And you with me somehow
Together
In our dream world finding trip
Forever

So, you know me now
And I'm so bared beside you
Even living so far still
Yet close enough
To feel your breath inside me

I can't live without you

I don't like your silence
you know
and I don't feel so comfortable
anymore
but maybe you have some reason
to be like this,
there is not any problem for me
that we can't meet
I know as well as you
that it can be difficult
but I love you
and my life really started
from the time you came but
if you don't feel good with me
anymore
you can go
away

Oh no please stay
Forget it what I just said
Never go away
Please stay

I need you so much
To live
You are this one for me
Who I can trust and love
and understand
and be real with
Please don't go
How I love you
How I love
Every single inch of you
Your every thought
You are my love
You are the part of me
Don't forget it
You understand me well
You can accept me as I'm
Even this what you said at the start
About all these mythologies around
You don't believe in
Makes me sure
That we are both as one

You can play and live as me
You can understand everything
All I want to do
Is just to dance with you
So, please stay
And come to me someday
I want this so much
I can't imagine my life without
You
Here inside my heart and soul
Here within all dreams I have
Because of you

Even if for a while

If I wish to be sure something on this world
It's you my love,
but you know too that
even if you don't have too much to offer to me
it's all right too,
it's enough to believe
it's enough just to live by this
so long as it is possible,
if I say be real with me
it is just that I wish you here
to be with me so open
and familiar and just as you are
I wish to believe in your heart
and your words
always so sweet to me
but you know there wont be any consequences
if you don't,
even if it's all nothing but dream
I still appreciate that you came
to me just to light my life
even if for a while

All we run for

Maybe all what we want and we run for
are these butterflies we feel inside

with this right one?
Even if you know

that you wont feel this forever
but still

you can't waste this what you can get,
this what you feel at the moment

he came
so you run and then
you long for this again.

And this how it works - love
pleasure
and prize for this
is this longing
for another while
you have to wait for
too long
not important

if you wait a day or a month or years
It's always too long
When you are in love

Don't miss me

You say you miss me,
So why don't you come?
If you miss me, my love
So please don't
Just come to me
You know how I love
Your voice
And every touch of your
Beautiful shining soul

So please just come
Every time you need this
Every time you want
I'm always for you
As you know

Just
Don't forget it
My boy

Some special meeting during a night

Not great dancer you are
You said
But with the man as you
It's enough
If you just watch
And then I'm glad
To dance with another man
Just feeling your eyes on me
And I'm fine somehow
So joyful inside
For the man like you
Just to be near is enough
To feel good
So thank you
To be so close
For this special moment
To remember
Thank you
To be my choice
And for this little voice
I have had inside
Just being by your side
For a while

More real be

All you are able to
Are these sweet lies you do
That's how you live
And I love it but I wish
Something more I think
Is it the end?
I don't know
Just a break I suppose
Just kind of calmness
When I'm waiting
For a miracle
You could bring to my heart
If you would only try
To be more real than you are
Right now

I wish to know more you

How I wish I could
Know you better
My love
But I don't want to ask
About all things
You do
Because already I know
You
Good enough to be sure
What are these answers
You could tell me
But still kind of mystery you are for me
Still so hungry of your thoughts I have to be
Because you are silent enough
To be sure only - your love
Nothing more
How I wish to see
All your soul
Talking freely to me
During a night during a day
And in our entire dream we live in still
Just listening your voice I wish here
Just reading your soul
Is all I need
My dear

Still together

So, you are my muse
But I'm not yours
Is it not beautiful what could happen
To this little artist that lives inside my soul
Is it not terrible for a woman I'm?
Oh baby all the time this mix of emotions
I feel inside thinking of you
But I'm nothing but me
So in love with you still
So I don't have any choice
I walk through my life with you
Inside my heart
For good and bad
For light and for dark
Colors
Of our lives
Still together...

Some moment in life

The only moment
that is really sweet
and worth to live
is this
when you say
I'm so special,
beautiful, unique
and that you need me,
want me, love me
and I believe
that it's true
This is the moment
I wish to live forever
When I'm smiling to you
swimming merrily in this charm
which you let me drown in
because life is just as you see your self
and someone else too
some little game you came
to enjoy

Invisible hope

I know
That you are
Quite invisible
In my life still
But these little
Touches
I have from you
In time
Mean to me more
Than all my world
And this hope
For you soon
Is all
I really long
And live for

You just fit to me

You are not too bad
and not too good
You just perfectly fit to my soul
And you make me feel the way I love
That's all what I need to be sure
That you and me is exactly this
What I want

I love this sweet madness I drawn

Are you sure my love that all we feel here
Is not but simple illusion of our heart?
And maybe we shouldn't meet at all
To not crash this sweet dream we own?

I feel so good in this lovely madness I have
I do not want to lose it
or lost any touch of yours
I do not want wake up to real life
I just want to believe in you and me
And live with this charm all the time
And feel you beside me
As I do now

It's so easy now

How it is easy now
To sing my ancient whipping song of love
When you are waiting for me on the other side of this dream
With open arms
No real longings I feel inside my heart
Either wanting to be loved
If I feel and I believe in us
Someday together
So close

My love how I'm glad that you came to my heart
To live here inside

So little you

There is so little you in my life still
How can I be sure that you are real?
How to believe in this love here?
I don't know my sweet man but what can I do
I still wish that all you said to me is true
I still find the light in this way
And this what I love to believe
Is this little dream we have here
That you and me is all
What we really need
Am I wrong?
Tell me

With or without you

You are never sure
If you take a prime
Or you are just a little piece
Of a great mystery
That is going on
When you take a part in it
And when you are gone
This moment of touch
This moment of smile
Is this what you really have
Then the show goes on
With or without you at all
Though you can always come back
To feel again that you are inside
Of this great book of life
And then you believe again that
It's you who holds the key
Of my soul and heart

Hey you

Hey you
Another lover of mine
Yesterday you said you love
So hard you want me
And today
I disappeared?
All signs of me
Are gone suddenly
I don't know
What to think
Have I done something?
I know something missed
Between you and me
Something real maybe?
The topic to feel alive
For a long time?
We are not able to go deeper
So we go out
It's so natural
As life

It was just a dream

So you don't want
This in real
All it was
Nothing but dream
Once again
I was naive
It's all right too
I can understand you
It was just a dream
And it's time to wake up
Again

Should remember

What to think of you now
My sweet one
If you do everything
That I'd stop believe in you and me
What makes you so extremely busy
To not leave me any sight of you anymore
To change your number phone
Just before my visit to your place?
Oh please come on
Why you do it to me, my love?
I thought I mean something for you
But maybe I was wrong
Why honestly you can't say
That you don't want
To see me in reality
That all fun maybe
Between you and me
Is only here
In our dream moon landing trip
Especially if we don't need
To meet too often
To not absorb each other too much
In our busy lives
Oh yes my love, I know
That sometimes we afraid
To face some real things
Or we simply lost some energy
To take it, to go on
Or to meet each other
As right now
I don't have force enough
To let you believe in this no more
I'll stay in my own world
There is no chance now
For more
If you don't wish it'd happen my love
Even if you always say
How much you do
These are nothing but words I know
Some lies you use
To caress my soul
Nothing more
It's nothing more
Yes, I should remember...

You and me

May it be just imagination
You and me?
May it be all just mind creation
Loving here?
We never touch, we never see
So how it can be
To feel you so much
In me
Why can't I stop to think of you
My love?
Why all my life
Is running around you
Right now
Even if you seems to
Walk away into the silence
If all you said was just to please me
If all you said was nothing
You really meant
So why, why
I miss your words and you
Right now
I can fill my life by thousand
Beautiful romances
But no one can take your place
No one can create this story
Of you and me
Don't you know this?
Don't you believe
That you and me
Is something different
That you and me
Is this dream I wish to live
Forever in
That you and me
Is all I want to believe in

Our home is here

It's so nice you have been back
In the form you like the most
My love
As some sweet little answer
For the basic question of my own soul
Now all is going on the way it was before
Just don't tell me anymore
How much you need to see me
Just don't ask me to come
Because I know
You don't want this at all
Our home is here
Forever and never we change this
It's good to live here for us
So please never say such lies
As before
Because I don't want
To be fool anymore
By your pretty charming words
And this hope for something more
I feel good here and I never want any change
No, no I wish to dream of you
Right here and more
But never ever want to see you
In real world

Let me dream then...

If love is nothing but illusion of the heart
so let me live in this dream forever
let me believe still
that you and me
is we
Don't wake me up
I love to dream like that
Don't wake me up
I want to sing my song
Till the end of love

Note from the author

My beautiful stranger thank you to come into my life for good as a dream and as a real man too I know that this together journey through the world will be so special as it is right now
forever

To my FC
With Love

Yours Anna

www.ingramcontent.com/pod-product-compliance
Lightning Source LLC
Chambersburg PA
CBHW072009060426

42446CB00042B/2278